Heroes for Young Readers

Written by Renee Taft Meloche
Illustrated by Bryan Pollard

Adoniram Judson
Amy Carmichael
Bethany Hamilton
Betty Greene
Brother Andrew
Cameron Townsend
Corrie ten Boom
C. S. Lewis
David Livingstone
Eric Liddell
George Müller

Gladys Aylward
Hudson Taylor
Ida Scudder
Jim Elliot
Jonathan Goforth
Loren Cunningham
Lottie Moon
Mary Slessor
Nate Saint
Nick Vujicic
William Carey

Heroes of History for Young Readers

Written by Renee Taft Meloche
Illustrated by Bryan Pollard

Daniel Boone
Clara Barton
George Washington
George Washington Carver
Louis Zamperini
Meriwether Lewis

*Heroes for Young Readers Activity Guides and audio CDs
are also available. See the back of this book for more information.*

www.HeroesThenAndNow.com

HEROES FOR YOUNG READERS

GEORGE MÜLLER

Faith to Feed Ten Thousand

Written by Renee Taft Meloche
Illustrated by Bryan Pollard

P.O. BOX 55787 SEATTLE, WA 98155

George Müller was a minister
    in eighteen thirty-three.
One day he strolled the streets of England
    feeling fancy-free.

He jumped over the puddles from
    the rain the night before.
He whistled as he walked and wondered
    what the future bore.

A carriage passed and water splashed
    his face, which made it gritty.
George did not care, for soon, he knew,
    he'd leave this crowded city.

Though George had come from Prussia
    (it's called Germany today),
he'd tired of tea and visiting
    and did not want to stay.

He'd lived for months in Bristol among
    squalor and disease
and thought it would be challenging
    to serve God overseas.

And recently he got the money
    he'd been waiting for
to serve God as a missionary
    on another shore.

He pushed past Bristol's poorest part
    along the cobbled street.
He hardly saw the beggars who
    were wanting food to eat.

But then a little girl approached,
    dressed in a gunnysack.
She carried a small toddler, who
    was riding piggyback.

Her dirt-streaked face looked up at him
    as she so shyly said,
"Can you please spare a shilling, sir?
    My ma and pa are dead."

George crouched beside the girl, who looked
no more than five years old.
Her brother had a runny nose
and shivered from the cold.

She said her name was Emily,
    and then, with great delight,
she spelled her name for George and got
    a shilling for the night.

George placed it in her unwashed hand.
    She straightened, feeling proud,
and hitched her brother higher up
    while heading toward the crowd.

George worried as he watched her
    disappearing out of sight.
Where would she go? What would she eat?
    Where would she sleep that night?

He felt so sad, his future plans
    completely changed that day.
He'd stay in England helping kids
    who had no place to stay.

So George, together with his wife,
    began a breakfast club.
Soon thirty kids attended from
    the streets and local pub.

They sat on apple boxes. Not
    one single child stirred
when George began to read aloud
    from God's own holy Word.

They ate big bowls of oatmeal, which
    they gobbled happily,
and shoveled spoons of sugar in
    their warm, delicious tea.

Now many poor in Bristol weren't
    as fortunate as they,
but lived within the poorhouse walls—
    an awful place to stay—
where husbands, wives, and children all
    were forced to live their lives
apart from one another, working
    hard there to survive.

A baby boy named William had
    been born one morning there.
His parents died when he was small,
    yet no one seemed to care.

Wherever little William went
    there scurried rats and mice.
At night he hardly slept a wink—
    his bed had fleas and lice.

Along with many others, William
        hoped to get away.
He told a lie about an aunt
        inviting him to stay.

So William went out on his own—
        now homeless on the street.
He searched through bits of trash in hope
        of finding food to eat.

He danced and sang some funny songs
        to earn a coin or two
and found more ways he could survive
        the older that he grew.

Now meanwhile George, not satisfied
        with what he had provided,
dreamed of a home for orphans and,
        with faith and hope, decided
one day in church that he'd announce
        what he was going to do:
"I know that God will help to make
        this orphanage come true."

"I will not ask for money but
        will ask the Lord in prayer
to meet the needs of every child
        who's placed within my care."

Some members thought his plan would fail.
        Their minds were filled with doubt:
Were there not more important things
        for God to care about?

Yet money, clothing, food, and sheets
        were given generously
to start a brand-new orphanage—
        a Christian ministry.

The years passed by. George was amazed
        as he watched God provide
five spacious houses for his orphans
        in the countryside.

Now William was a boy of twelve
        when he came there to stay.
So strange at first, it felt to him
        more like his home each day.

His placement in the school—since
        he could not read or write—
was in the kindergarten class.
        He studied hard each night.

And after many years he found
        a job as he had planned.
But just before he left George said,
        "My lad, give me your hand."

George placed a coin in his left palm,
        a Bible in his right.
"Hold tightly to God's Word," he said.
        "Don't let it out of sight."

"You'll find there's always something in
your other hand that way.
Yes, God will take good care of you,
and now, my boy, let's pray."

One morning in the orphanage,
     three hundred children met
and stood around the breakfast table,
     which was nicely set,
but yet they stared at empty plates
     and waited in that hall,
while George appeared relaxed although
     there was no food at all.

Surprisingly, George said to them,
     "Let's all please take a seat
and thank the Lord for giving us
     what we're about to eat."

Then suddenly a baker knocked
and came in with a tray.
"I could not sleep because I thought
you'd need this bread today."

Then while the children ate their fill
        of warm and tasty bread,
the milkman knocked. "My cart has broken
        down outside," he said.

"I must unload my milk so I
        can fix it properly.
Please take the bottles off my cart
        and drink them. They are free."

The children were amazed how God
        put food upon their plate,
right in the very nick of time
        and not a minute late.

George preached around the world and traveled
    in the U.S.A.
The orphans who'd grown up and moved
    there met him on his way.

And in New Zealand George spent all
    the time he could allow
with former street boy William—a
    beloved pastor now.

As George grew old, he settled down
        and spent his final days
surrounded by new orphans he
        could help in many ways.

He strolled along the garden paths
        and talked to children there
and told them Bible stories in
        the open English air.

At ninety-two George Müller died
    while sleeping peacefully.
He'd helped ten thousand orphans through
    his life, which we can see
was lived as an example of
    what each of us can do—
if we will put our faith in God
    and let Him use us too.

Wherever God may lead us, whether
    it be near or far,
as George discovered, through one girl:
    be helpful where you are.

Heroes for Young Readers and Heroes of History for Young Readers are based on the Christian Heroes: Then & Now and Heroes of History biographies by Janet & Geoff Benge. Don't miss out on these exciting, true adventures for ages 10 and up!

Christian Heroes: Then & Now

by Janet & Geoff Benge

Nate Saint: On a Wing and a Prayer
Paul Brand: Helping Hands
Rachel Saint: A Star in the Jungle
Rowland Bingham: Into Africa's Interior
Samuel Zwemer: The Burden of Arabia
Sundar Singh: Footprints Over the Mountains
Wilfred Grenfell: Fisher of Men
William Booth: Soup, Soap, and Salvation
William Carey: Obliged to Go

Heroes of History
by Janet & Geoff Benge

Abraham Lincoln: A New Birth of Freedom
Alan Shepard: Higher and Faster
Ben Carson: A Chance at Life
Benjamin Franklin: Live Wire
Billy Graham: America's Pastor
Captain John Smith: A Foothold in the New World
Christopher Columbus: Across the Ocean Sea
Clara Barton: Courage under Fire
Daniel Boone: Frontiersman
Davy Crockett: Ever Westward
Douglas MacArthur: What Greater Honor
George Washington: True Patriot
George Washington Carver: From Slave to Scientist
Harriet Tubman: Freedombound
John Adams: Independence Forever
Laura Ingalls Wilder: A Storybook Life
Meriwether Lewis: Off the Edge of the Map
Milton Hershey: More Than Chocolate
Orville Wright: The Flyer
Ronald Reagan: Destiny at His Side
Theodore Roosevelt: An American Original
Thomas Edison: Inspiration and Hard Work
William Penn: Liberty and Justice for All

Available in paperback, e-book, and audiobook formats.
Unit Study Curriculum Guides are available for each biography.